JUNIOR BIOS

Kristen Bell

BY NORA GARDINER

Enslow PUBLISHING

Please visit our website, www.enslow.com. For a free color catalog of all our high-quality books, call toll free 1-800-398-2504 or fax 1-877-980-4454.

Library of Congress Cataloging-in-Publication Data

Names: Gardiner, Nora, author.
Title: Kristen Bell / Nora Gardiner.
Description: New York : Enslow Publishing, 2022. | Series: Junior bios | Includes index.
Identifiers: LCCN 2020034778 | ISBN 9781978522688 (library binding) | ISBN 9781978522664 (paperback) | ISBN 9781978522671 (6 pack) | ISBN 9781978522695 (ebook)
Subjects: LCSH: Bell, Kristen, 1980-—Juvenile literature. | Actors—United States—Biography—Juvenile literature.
Classification: LCC PN2287.B4133 G38 2022 | DDC 791.4302/8092 [B]—dc23
LC record available at https://lccn.loc.gov/2020034778

First Edition

Published in 2022 by
Enslow Publishing
29 E. 21st Street
New York, NY 10010

Designer: Deanna Paternostro
Editor: Kate Mikoley

Photo credits: Cover, p. 1 (Kristen Bell) Jim Spellman/Contributor/Getty Images Entertainment/Getty Images; cover, p. 1 (photo frame) Aleksandr Andrushkiv/Shutterstock.com; marble texture used throughout HardtIllustrations/Shutterstock.com; lined paper texture used throughout Mtsaride/Shutterstock.com; watercolor texture used throughout solarbird/Shutterstock.com; p. 5 Brian Ach/Contributor/WireImage/Getty Images; p. 7 Lee Celano/Contributor/WireImage/Getty Images; p. 9 Amanda Edwards/Stringer/Getty Images Entertainment/Getty Images; p. 11 CBS Photo Archive/Contributor/CBS/Getty Images; p. 13 Michael Caulfield/Staff/WireImage/Getty Images; p. 15 Allen Berezovsky/Contributor/WireImage/Getty Images; p. 17 Handout/Handout/Getty Images Entertainment/Getty Images; p. 19 Jesse Grant/Stringer/Getty Images Entertainment/Getty Images.

Printed in the United States of America

CPSIA compliance information: Batch #CSENS22: For further information contact Enslow Publishing, New York, New York, at 1-800-398-2504.

Contents

Words in the glossary appear in **bold** type the first time they are used in the text.

Bell's Beginning

As a child, Kristen Bell knew she wanted to be an actor. By her early twenties, she was already appearing on Broadway. It wasn't long before she was landing TV and movie roles, or parts. Today, Kristen Bell is a famous actor, as well as a singer, writer, and much more.

Helping people is also important to Kristen. She uses her fame to fight for causes she believes in. She's worked with and supported numerous organizations, or groups. She even helped start a company that uses its money to help get lifesaving treatments to children in need.

KRISTEN LOVES ANIMALS. SHE HAS WORKED WITH SEVERAL GROUPS THAT HELP ANIMALS. SHE HAS ALSO BEEN A VEGETARIAN, OR SOMEONE WHO DOESN'T EAT MEAT, SINCE SHE WAS 11.

Kristen was born on July 18, 1980, in Huntington Woods, Michigan. Huntington Woods is a **suburb** of the largest city in Michigan—Detroit. She grew up around this area. By the time Kristen was a teenager, she was already working as an actor, having appeared in several TV commercials. She worked with an agent, or a person whose job it is to help actors get jobs.

FACTS BEHIND THE FIGURE

Kristen was always interested in performing. As a kid, she would memorize TV commercials and songs she heard, repeating them out loud to entertain those around her.

KRISTEN'S MOM, LORELEI, SHOWN HERE WITH KRISTEN, WORKED AS A NURSE. KRISTEN'S DAD, TOM, WAS A TV NEWS DIRECTOR.

In high school, Kristen was very interested in theater, appearing in several school musicals. She even starred as the main character, Dorothy, in her high school's production of *The Wizard of Oz*!

Broadway Is Calling

In New York City, many famous theaters are on or around a street called Broadway. Shows at these theaters often become very famous and being cast in one is usually considered a big accomplishment for an actor.

After high school, Kristen decided to move to New York City and go to New York University. There, she studied musical theater at the Tisch School of the Arts. In 2001, she got her first big break in acting when she was cast in a musical production of *The Adventures of Tom Sawyer* on Broadway!

KRISTEN HAD HER FIRST MOVIE ROLE IN 1998 IN A MOVIE CALLED *POLISH WEDDING*. THE MOVIE WAS FILMED NEAR HER HOMETOWN IN DETROIT, MICHIGAN. HER ROLE WAS SMALL AND **UNCREDITED**.

FACTS BEHIND THE FIGURE

In 2001, Kristen was also in an off-Broadway show. This is a show at a smaller theater that is usually less well-known than a Broadway show. In 2002, she was back on Broadway in a play called *The Crucible*.

Off to Mars

Soon after her job in *The Crucible* was done, Kristen moved to Los Angeles, California. Once she was there, it didn't take her long to land several small roles on TV shows.

In 2004, Kristen started a job that would change her life. Though she had already been working in entertainment for years, she was not yet the recognizable star she is today. That changed when she started playing the lead character on *Veronica Mars*. In this TV show, Kristen played Veronica, a young detective who started solving crimes when she was still a teenager.

KRISTEN WAS THE FIRST OF AROUND 100 ACTRESSES TO TRY OUT FOR THE ROLE OF VERONICA MARS.

FACTS BEHIND THE FIGURE

Veronica Mars was on TV for three seasons between 2004 and 2007. During this time, it gained a serious following of **devoted** fans. Kristen returned to play her character in a 2014 movie, as well as on another season of the TV show in 2019!

Speak Up!

During her time on *Veronica Mars*, Kristen also worked on several other projects. By the time the show ended in 2007, she was well-known in Hollywood. Kristen didn't waste any time finding her next regular TV role.

The same year *Veronica Mars* ended, Kristen started her new job on the TV show *Gossip Girl*. This role was a bit different from Veronica, as Kristen wasn't actually shown in the show. She voiced the **narrator**, also known to viewers as Gossip Girl. Her voice framed each episode. Just as the name suggests, her character gossips, or talks about the personal lives of the show's characters.

KRISTEN LENT HER VOICE TO ANOTHER PROJECT IN 2009, VOICING CORA IN THE **ANIMATED** FILM *ASTRO BOY*.

FACTS BEHIND THE FIGURE

During her time working on *Gossip Girl*, Kristen also regularly appeared on a popular TV show called *Heroes*. She was also in several movies, including *Forgetting Sarah Marshall*, *Couples Retreat*, and *Get Him to the Greek*.

Is It Cold in Here?

By 2013, Kristen was no stranger to voice acting. Now, it was time for her to be the voice of what would become one of the best-known Disney characters—Anna from *Frozen*. Kristen won several awards for her part in this movie, and the film won two Academy Awards—the biggest awards in film.

In Her Own Words

"Music has been a very big part of my life for a long, long time ... I realized I liked music so much and when you could be a storyteller while you were singing, that was the best of both worlds."

WHEN IT CAME OUT, *FROZEN* MADE MORE MONEY THAN ANY OTHER ANIMATED MOVIE HAD MADE UP UNTIL THAT TIME.

Kristen did more than just talk for Anna—she sang too! Even though she grew up doing musical theater and sang on Broadway, many people didn't know Kristen could sing and were surprised to learn it was really her singing in the movie.

Frozen was so successful that Disney decided to make a sequel, or a follow-up to the first movie. *Frozen II* came out in 2019, and Kristen was back as the voice of Anna. This film was even more successful than the first movie and became the new highest-earning animated movie at the time. It was also the third biggest movie of 2019!

FACTS BEHIND THE FIGURE

Kristen often talks about her own **anxiety** and **depression** in hopes that it can help others dealing with similar feelings. One *Frozen II* song was inspired by what Kristen tells herself to do when she is feeling down or doesn't know what to do: "The Next Right Thing."

ANNA'S OLDER SISTER, ELSA, IS VOICED BY IDINA MENZEL, WHO FIRST BECAME FAMOUS FOR HER ROLES IN SEVERAL BROADWAY SHOWS.

In *Frozen II*, Anna deals with personal issues in her life, such as being unsure of what to do. Kristen has said she used her own life experiences for inspiration for playing the character going through these issues.

Doing Good

From 2016 to 2020, Kristen starred as the main character on a popular TV show called *The Good Place*. In the show, Kristen's character tries to figure out what it means to be good.

In Her Own Words

"My goal in life is to spread more joy and reduce suffering any way I can. It makes me feel good when I lay my head on the pillow at night that I could be of service to someone else."

IN 2020, KRISTEN AND HER *FROZEN* COSTAR JOSH GAD SOLD SPECIAL HATS THAT FEATURED A JOKE FROM *FROZEN II*. ALL MONEY MADE FROM THE SALES WAS GIVEN TO CHARITY.

In real life, Kristen does a lot of good. In 2013, she launched a company called This Saves Lives along with several friends. The company sells granola bars, known as This Bar Saves Lives, and uses the **proceeds** to provide a special food packed full of **nutrients** to children who are fighting **malnutrition**. This special food can save their lives!

Keeping Busy

Kristen is married to an actor named Dax Shepard. They have two daughters. In 2019, Kristen and Dax launched their own line of baby products called Hello Bello. The products are made with plants and are meant to be more affordable than some similar products.

In 2020, Kristen came out with a children's book. She wrote the book, called *The World Needs More Purple People*, with her friend Benjamin Hart. It's about finding common ground with other people.

What's next for a star who has sung on Broadway, starred on TV, and belted her heart out as a Disney character? Only time will tell!

Kristen's Timeline

1980: KRISTEN IS BORN ON JULY 18.

1998: KRISTEN APPEARS IN HER FIRST MOVIE, *POLISH WEDDING*.

2001: KRISTEN IS IN *THE ADVENTURES OF TOM SAWYER* ON BROADWAY.

2002: KRISTEN IS IN *THE CRUCIBLE* ON BROADWAY.

2004: KRISTEN STARTS PLAYING THE LEAD CHARACTER IN *VERONICA MARS*.

2007: *VERONICA MARS* ENDS—FOR NOW!

KRISTEN STARTS VOICING THE NARRATOR IN *GOSSIP GIRL*.

2013: *FROZEN* COMES OUT.

THIS SAVES LIVES IS LAUNCHED.

2014: *VERONICA MARS: THE MOVIE* COMES OUT.

2016: *THE GOOD PLACE* FIRST AIRS.

2019: KRISTEN AND DAX START THEIR LINE, HELLO BELLO.

KRISTEN RETURNS AS VERONICA FOR A NEW SEASON OF *VERONICA MARS*.

FROZEN II COMES OUT.

2020: *THE WORLD NEEDS MORE PURPLE PEOPLE* IS PUBLISHED.

Glossary

animated Consisting of drawings or computer images that appear to move.

anxiety A serious fear or nervousness about what might happen.

depression A medical condition in which a person feels very sad, hopeless, and unimportant.

devoted Having a strong loyalty or love for something.

malnutrition A condition of poor health that comes from not eating or having access to enough nutrient-rich food.

narrator The person who tells a story.

nutrient Something a living thing needs to grow and stay alive.

proceeds Money made from sales.

suburb An area outside of but close to a bigger city.

uncredited Not named as one of the people who worked on something.

For More Information

Books

Canasi, Brittany. *So You Wanna Be: An Actor*. North Mankato, MN: Rourke Educational Media, 2019.

March, Julia. *Frozen 2: The Magical Guide*. New York, NY: DK Publishing, 2019.

Wood, Alix. *Be an Actor*. New York, NY: PowerKids Press, 2018.

Websites

Disney: Frozen
frozen.disney.com/
Watch videos and learn more about the characters of *Frozen* here.

Kristen Bell Biography
www.biography.com/actor/kristen-bell
Head to this website to learn even more about Kristen.

Publisher's note to educators and parents: Our editors have carefully reviewed these websites to ensure that they are suitable for students. Many websites change frequently, however, and we cannot guarantee that a site's future contents will continue to meet our high standards of quality and educational value. Be advised that students should be closely supervised whenever they access the internet.

Index